Cabin Retreat

Skill Level

 EASY

Size

Approximately 42 x 54 inches

Materials

- Red Heart Super Saver
  medium (worsted)
  weight yarn (7 oz/364
  yds/196g per skein):
  - 4 skeins #334 buff *(A)*
  - 1 skein each #365 coffee *(B)*
    and #332 ranch red *(C)*
- Size H/8/5mm crochet hook or
  size needed to obtain gauge
- Tapestry needle
- Stitch marker

Gauge

From point to point, 1 horizontal
  pattern rep = 6 inches

Special Stitch

Cluster (cl): Keeping last lp of each
dc on hook, dc in sk sc indicated,
sk next 2 sk sc, dc in next sk sc,
yo and draw through all 3 lps
on hook.

Instructions

Row 1 (RS): With A, ch 217 loosely;
sc in 2nd ch from hook and in
next 14 chs, ch 2; *sc in next 14
chs, sk next ch, dc in next ch, sk
next ch, sc in next 14 chs, ch 2;
rep from * 5 times; sc in last 15
chs. Fasten off.

Row 2: Hold piece with WS facing you; sk first sc, with B make slip knot on hook and join with sc in next sc; *sc in next 4 sc, ch 1, sk next sc, [sc in next sc, ch 1, sk next sc] twice; sc in next 4 sc, in next ch-2 sp work (sc, ch 2, sc); sc in next 4 sc, ch 1, sk next sc, [sc in next sc, ch 1, sk next sc] twice; sc in next 4 sc, sk next sc, sc in next st, sk next sc; rep from * 5 times; sc in next 4 sc, ch 1, sk next sc, [sc in next sc, ch 1, sk next sc] twice; sc in next 4 sc, in next ch-2 sp work (sc, ch 2, sc); sc in next 4 sc, ch 1, sk next sc, [sc in next sc, ch 1, sk next sc] twice; sc in next 5 sc. Fasten off, leaving last sc unworked.

Row 3: Hold piece with RS facing you; sk first sc, with A make slip knot on hook and join with sc in next sc; *sc in next 3 sc, dc in next sk st on 2nd row below, sk st behind dc just made, [sc in next sc, dc in next sk st on 2nd row below, sk st behind dc just made] twice; sc in next 5 sc, in next ch-2 sp work (sc, ch 2, sc); sc in next 5 sc, dc in next sk st on 2nd row below, sk st behind dc just made, [sc in next sc, dc in next sk st on 2nd row below, sk st behind dc just made] twice; sc in next 3 sc, sk next sc, sc in next sc, sk next sc; rep from * 5 times; sc in next 3 sc, dc in next sk st on 2nd row below, sk st behind dc just made, [sc in next sc, dc in next sk st on 2nd row below, sk st behind dc just made] twice; sc in next 5 sc, in next ch-2 sp work (sc, ch 2, sc); sc in next 5 sc, dc in next sk st on 2nd row below, sk st behind dc just made, [sc in next sc, dc in next sk st on 2nd row below, sk st behind dc just made] twice; sc in next 4 sc. Fasten off, leaving last sc unworked.

Rows 4–7: [Work rows 2 and 3] twice.

Row 8: Hold piece with WS facing you; sk first sc, with A make slip knot on hook and join with sc in next sc, sc in next 13 sts, in next ch-2 sp work (sc, ch 2, sc); *sc in next 13 sts, sk next st, sc in next st, sk next st, sc in next 13 sts, in next ch-2 sp work (sc, ch 2, sc); rep from * 5 times; sc in next 14 sts. Fasten off, leaving last sc unworked.

Row 9: Hold piece with RS facing you; sk first sc, with A make slip knot on hook and join with sc in next sc, sc in next 13 sts, in next ch-2 sp work (sc, ch 2, sc); *sc in next 13 sts, sk next st, sc in next st, sk next st, sc in next 13 sts, in next ch-2 sp work (sc, ch 2, sc); rep from * 5 times; sc in next 14 sc. Fasten off, leaving last sc unworked.

Row 10: Hold piece with WS facing you; sk first sc, with C make slip knot on hook and join with sc in next sc; *sc in next 4 sts, ch 4, sk next 3 sc, sc in next 5 sc, ch 1, sk next sc, in next ch-2 sp work (sc, ch 2, sc); ch 1, sk next sc, sc in next 5 sc, ch 4, sk next 3 sc, sc in next 4 sc, sk next sc, sc in next sc, sk next sc; rep from * 5 times; sc in next 4 sts, ch 4, sk next 3 sc, sc in next 5 sc, ch 1, sk next sc, in next ch-2 sp work (sc, ch 2, sc); ch 1, sk next sc, sc in next 5 sc, ch 4, sk next 3 sc, sc in next 5 sc. Fasten off, leaving last sc unworked.

Row 11: Hold piece with RS facing you; sk first sc, with A make slip knot on hook and join with sc in next sc; *sc in next 2 sts, ch 1, sk next sc, dc in next 3 sk sc on 2nd row below, ch 1, sk next sc, sc in next 3 sc, ch 1, sk next sc, dc in sk sc on 2nd row below, sk st behind dc just made, sc in next sc, in next ch-2 sp work (sc, ch 2, sc); sc in next sc, dc in next sk sc on 2nd row below, sk st behind dc just made, ch 1, sk next sc, sc in next 3 sc, ch 1, sk next sc, dc in next 3

sk sc on 2nd row below, ch 1, sk next sc, sc in next 2 sc, sk next sc, sc in next sc, sk next sc; rep from * 5 times; sc in next 2 sts, ch 1, sk next sc, dc in next 3 sk sc on 2nd row below, ch 1, sk next sc, sc in next 3 sc, ch 1, sk next sc, dc in sk sc on 2nd row below, sk st behind dc just made, sc in next sc, in next ch-2 sp work (sc, ch 2, sc); sc in next sc, dc in next sk sc on 2nd row below, sk st behind dc just made, ch 1, sk next sc, sc in next 3 sc, ch 1, sk next sc, dc in next 3 sk sc on 2nd row below, ch 1, sk next sc, sc in next 3 sc. Fasten off, leaving last sc unworked.

Row 12: Hold piece with WS facing you; sk first sc, with C make slip knot on hook and join with sc in next sc; ch 1, sk next sc; *working behind next ch-1 sp, dc in sk sc on 2nd row below, sk st in front of dc just made, sc in next 3 sts, working behind next ch-1 sp, dc in next sk sc on 2nd row below, ch 4, sk next 3 sc, working behind next ch-1 sp, dc in skipped sc on 2nd row below, sc in next 3 sts, in next ch-2 sp work (sc, ch 2, sc); sc in next 3 sts, working behind next ch-1 sp, dc in next sk sc on 2nd row below, ch 4, sk next 3 sc, working behind next ch-1 sp, dc in next sk sc on 2nd row below, sc in next 3 sts, working behind next ch-1 sp, dc in next sk sc on 2nd row below, ch 1, sk next 2 sc, sc in next sc, ch 1, sk next 2 sc; rep from * 5 times; working behind next ch, dc in sk sc on 2nd row below, sk st in front of dc just made, sc in next 3 sts, working behind next ch-1 sp, dc in next sk sc on 2nd row below, ch 4, sk next 3 sc, working behind next ch-1 sp, dc in skipped sc on 2nd row below, sc in next 3 sts, in next ch-2 sp work (sc, ch 2, sc); sc in next 3 sts, working behind next ch-1 sp, dc in next sk sc on 2nd row below, ch 4, sk next 3 sc, working behind next ch-1 sp, dc

   American School of Needlework • Berne, Indiana 46711 • DRGnetwork.com

in next sk sc on 2nd row below, sc in next 3 sts, working behind next ch-1 sp, dc in next sk sc on 2nd row below, ch 1, sk next sc, sc in next sc. Fasten off, leaving last sc unworked.

Row 13: Hold piece with RS facing you; sk first sc, with A make slip knot on hook and join with sc in next sc; *sc in next 5 sts, working in front of next ch-4 sp, dc in next 3 sk sc on 2nd row below, sc in next 5 sts, in next ch-2 sp work (sc, ch 3, sc); sc in next 5 sts, working in front of next ch-4 sp, dc in next 3 sk sc on 2nd row below, sc in next 5 sts, working in front of next 2 ch-1 sps, **cl** *(see Special Stitch)* in first and 4th sk sc on 2nd row below; rep from * 5 times; sc in next 5 sts, working in front of next ch-4 sp, dc in next 3 sk sc on 2nd row below, sc in next 5 sts, in next ch-2 sp work (sc, ch 3, sc); sc in next 5 sts, working in front of next ch-4 sp, dc in next 3 sk sc on 2nd row below, sc in next 5 sts, working in front of next ch-1 sp, dc in next sk sc on 2nd row below. Fasten off, leaving last sc unworked.

Row 14: Hold piece with WS facing you; sk first sc, with A make slip knot on hook and join with sc in next sc, sc in next 13 sts, in next ch-3 sp work (sc, ch 2, sc); *sc in next 13 sts, sk next st, sc in next st, sk next st, sc in next 13 sts, in next ch-3 sp work (sc, ch 2, sc); rep from * 5 times; sc in next 14 sts. Fasten off, leaving last sc unworked.

Row 15: Hold piece with RS facing you; sk first sc, with A, make slip knot on hook and join with sc in next sc, sc in next 13 sts, in next ch-2 sp work (sc, ch 2, sc); *sc in next 13 sts, sk next st, sc in next st, sk next st, sc in next 13 sts, in next ch-2 sp work (sc, ch 2, sc); rep from * 5 times; sc in next 14 sts. Fasten off, leaving last st unworked.

Rep rows 2–15 until piece measures approximately 52 inches from beg. Then rep rows 2–6.
Weave in all ends.

Edging
Hold piece with RS facing you and last row worked to left; with A make slip knot on hook and join with sc in unused sc at beg of row 1; 2 sc in same sc; working across side in unused sc at ends of rows, sc in each rem row; mark last sc made; ch 1; working across last row, sc in first sc, ch 1, sc in next 4 sc; *working in front of next ch-1 sp, dc in next sk st on 2nd row below, [sc in next sc, working in front of next ch-1 sp, dc in next sk st on 2nd row below] twice; sc in next 5 sc, in next ch-2 sp work (sc, ch 2, sc); sc in next 5 sc; working in front of next ch-1 sp, dc in next sk st on 2nd row below, [sc in next sc, working in front of next ch-1 sp, dc in next sk st on 2nd row below] twice; sc in next 3 sc, sk next sc, sc in next sc, sk next sc, sc in next 3 sc; rep from * 6 times; working in front of next ch-1 sp, dc in next sk st on 2nd row below, [sc in next sc, working in front of next ch-1 sp, dc in next sk st on 2nd row below] twice; sc in next 5 sc, in next ch-2 sp work (sc,

ch 2, sc); sc in next 5 sc; working in front of next ch-1 sp, dc in next sk st on 2nd row below, [sc in next sc, working in front of next ch, dc in next sk st on 2nd row below] twice; sc in next 4 sc, ch 1, sc in last sc, ch 1, working across next side in unused sc at end of rows, sc in each row to row 1; 3 sc in end of row 1.
Fasten off and weave in ends.

Border
Hold piece with RS facing you; with A make slip knot on hook and join with sc in marked sc; sc in next ch-1 sp, in next sc, in next ch-1 sp and in next 15 sts; 3 sc in next ch-2 sp; [sc in next 13 sts, sk next sc, sc in next sc, sk next sc, sc in next 13 sts, 3 sc in next ch-2 sp] 7 times; sc in next 15 sts, sc in next ch-1 sp, in next sc, in next ch-1 sp and in each sc across to last sc of Edging; in last sc work (sc, ch 1, 2 sc); working across next side in unused lps of beg ch, sc in next 14 lps, sk next 2 lps, sc in next 14 lps, [3 sc in next lp, sc in next 14 lps, sk next 2 lps, sc in next 14 lps] 7 times; working across next side of Edging, in first sc work (2 sc, ch 1, sc); sc in each sc to first sc; join with sl st in first sc.
Fasten off and weave in ends. ●

Soft Sophistication

Skill Level

 ■■☐☐ EASY

Size

Approximately 37 x 50 inches
Note: This afghan is sized to cover both legs when seated.

Materials

• Red Heart Soft Yarn medium (worsted) weight yarn (5 oz/256 yds/140g per skein):
   4 skeins #9344 chocolate *(A)*
   2 skeins #9522 leaf *(B)*
   1 skein each #9518 teal *(C)* and #9114 honey *(D)*
• Size H/8/5mm crochet hook or size needed to obtain gauge
• Tapestry needle

Gauge

From point to point, 1 horizontal pattern rep = 5¼ inches

Special Stitches

Cluster (cl): Ch 4, keeping last lp of each dc on hook, 2 dc in 4th ch from hook; yo and draw through all 3 lps on hook.
Shell: In st indicated work (sc, ch 2, dc in side of sc just made, dc).

Instructions

Row 1 (RS): With A, ch 179 loosely; dc in 5th ch from hook *(beg 4 sk chs count as a sk ch and a dc)*; sk next ch, dc in next ch; *[ch 1, sk next ch, dc in next ch] 3 times; in next ch work [dc, ch 1] twice; dc in same ch and in next ch; [ch 1, sk next ch, dc in next ch] 3 times; [sk next ch, dc in next ch] 4 times; rep from * 6 times; [ch 1, sk next ch, dc in next ch] 3 times; in next ch work [dc, ch 1] twice; dc in same ch and in next ch; [ch 1, sk next ch, dc in next ch] 3 times; [sk next ch, dc in next ch] twice. Fasten off.

Row 2: Hold piece with WS facing you; with B make slip knot on hook and join with sc in first dc; ch 1, sk next dc, sc in next dc, [ch 1, sc in next dc] 3 times; *ch 1, sk next dc, sc in next ch-1 sp, **cl** *(see Special Stitches)*; ch 1, sk next dc, sc in next ch-1 sp, ch 1, sk next dc, sc in next dc, [ch 1, sc in next dc] 3 times; [ch 1, sk next dc, sc in next dc] twice; [ch 1, sc in next dc] 3 times; rep from * 6 times; ch 1, sk next dc, sc in next ch-1 sp, cl; ch 1, sk next dc, sc in next ch-1 sp, ch 1, sk next dc, sc in next dc, [ch 1, dc in next dc] 3 times; ch 1, sk next dc, sc in next ch of beg 4 sk chs. Fasten off.

Row 3: Hold piece with RS facing you; with A make slip knot on hook and join with dc in first sc; [sk next ch-1 sp, dc in next sc] twice; *[ch 1, sk next ch-1 sp, dc in next sc] 3 times; working behind next cl, in next sk dc on 2nd row below work [tr, ch 1] twice; tr in same dc; on working row, dc in next sc, [ch 1, sk next ch-1 sp, dc in next sc] 3 times; [sk next ch-1 sp, dc in next sc] 4 times; rep from * 6 times; [ch 1, sk next ch-1 sp, dc in next sc] 3 times; working behind next cl, in next sk dc on 2nd row below work [tr, ch 1] twice; tr in same dc; on working row, dc in next sc, [ch 1, sk next ch-1 sp, dc in next sc] 3 times; [sk next ch-1 sp, dc in next sc] twice. Fasten off.

Row 4: Hold piece with WS facing you; with B make slip knot on hook and join with sc in first dc; ch 1, sk next dc, sc in next dc, [ch 1, sk next ch-1 sp, sc in next st] twice; *cl; ch 1, sk next dc and next tr, sc in next ch-1 sp, cl; ch 1, sk next tr, sc in next ch-1 sp, cl; ch 1, sk next tr, next dc and next ch-1 sp, sc in next st, [ch 1, sk next st, sc in next st] 6 times; rep from * 6 times; cl; ch 1, sk next dc and next tr, sc in next ch-1 sp, cl; ch 1, sk next tr, sc in next ch-1 sp, cl; ch 1, sk next tr, next dc and next ch-1 sp, sc in next st, [ch 1, sk next ch-1 sp, sc in next dc] twice; ch 1, sk next dc, sc in next dc. Fasten off.

Row 5: Hold piece with RS facing you; with A make slip knot on hook and join with dc in first sc, [sk next ch-1 sp, dc in next sc] twice; *ch 1, sk next ch-1 sp, dc in next sc, ch 1, working behind next cl, tr in next sk dc on 2nd row below; ch 1, on working row, dc in next sc, working behind next cl, in sk tr on 2nd row below work [tr, ch 1] twice; tr in same sk tr; on working row, dc in next sc, ch 1, working behind next cl, tr in sk dc on 2nd row below; ch 1, on working row, dc in next sc, ch 1, sk next ch-1 sp, dc in next sc, [sk next ch-1 sp, dc in next sc] 4 times; rep from * 6 times; ch 1, sk next ch-1 sp, dc in next sc, ch 1, working behind next cl, tr in sk dc on 2nd row below; ch 1, on working row, dc in next sc, working behind next cl, in sk tr on 2nd row below work [tr, ch 1] twice; tr in same sk tr, on working row, dc in next sc, ch 1, working behind next cl, tr in sk dc on 2nd row below; ch 1, on working row, dc in next sc, ch 1, sk next ch-1 sp, dc in next sc, [sk next ch-1 sp, dc in next sc] twice. Fasten off.

Rows 6 & 7: Rep rows 4 and 5.

Row 8: Hold piece with WS facing you; with C make slip knot on hook and join with sc in first dc; ch 1, sk next dc, sc in next dc, [ch 1, sc in next dc] 3 times; *ch 1, sk next tr, sc in next ch-1 sp, cl; ch 1, sk next tr, sc in next ch-1 sp, ch 1, sk next tr, sc in next dc, ch 1, sc in next tr; [ch-1 sc in next dc] twice, [ch 1, sk next dc, sc in next dc] twice; ch 1, sc in next dc, ch-1 sc in next tr, ch-1 sc in next dc; rep from * 6 times; ch 1, sk next tr, sc in next ch-1 sp, cl; ch 1, sk next tr, sc in next ch-1 sp, ch 1, sk next tr, sc in next dc, ch 1, sc in next tr; [ch-1, sc in next dc] twice, ch 1, sk next dc, sc in next dc. Fasten off.

Row 9: Rep row 3.

Row 10: With C, rep row 4.

Row 11: Rep row 5.

Row 12: With C, rep row 4.

Row 13: Rep row 5.

Row 14: With D, rep row 8.

Row 15: Rep row 3.

Row 16: With D, rep row 4.

Row 17: Rep row 5.

Row 18: With D, rep row 4.

Row 19: Rep row 5.

Row 20: With B, rep row 8.

Rep rows 3–20 until piece measures approximately 47 inches from beg.

Rep rows 3–7.

Weave in all ends.

Edging

Hold afghan with RS facing you and last row worked at top; with A make slip knot on hook and join with sc in first dc in upper right-hand corner; ch 2, dc in side of joining sc, dc in same dc as joining sc made; [sk next 2 sts, **shell** (see Special Stitches) in next st] 3 times; sk next ch-1 sp, shell in next dc, sk next ch-1 sp; *[shell in next st, sk next 2 sts] twice; [sc in next st, sk next st] 3 times; shell in next ch-1 sp, [sk next 2 sts, shell in next st] twice; sk next ch-1 sp,

shell in next st, sk next ch-1 sp; rep from * 6 times; [shell in next st, sk next 2 sts] 3 times; shell in last dc; working across next side in ends of rows, sk first row, shell in next sc row; **sk next row, shell in next row; rep from ** to row 1; working across next side in unused lps of beg ch, shell in first lp; sk next lp, [shell in next lp, sk next 2 lps] twice; [sc in next lp, sk next lp] 3 times; [shell in next lp, sk next 2 lps] twice; ***[shell in next lp, sk next lp] twice; [shell in next lp, sk next 2 lps] twice; [sc in next lp, sk next lp] 3 times; [shell in next lp, sk next 2 lps] twice; rep from *** 3 times; shell in next lp; sk next lp, shell in last lp; working across next side in ends of rows, sk row 1; ****shell in next row, sk next row; rep from **** to joining sc; join with sl st in joining sc.

Fasten off and weave in ends. ●

Reversible Diamonds

Skill Level

■■□□ EASY

Size

Approximately 44 x 54 inches

Materials

- Red Heart Super Saver medium (worsted) weight yarn (7 oz/364 yds/198g per skein):
    - 4 skeins #313 Aran (A)
    - 3 skeins #362 spruce (B)
- Size H/8/5mm crochet hook or size needed to obtain gauge
- Tapestry needle
- Stitch marker

Gauge

From point to point, 3 horizontal pattern reps = 12½ inches

Instructions

Row 1 (WS): With B, ch 231 loosely; sc in 2nd ch from hook and in next 9 chs, ch 2; *sc in next 9 chs, sk next ch, dc in next ch, sk next ch, sc in next 9 chs, ch 2; rep from * 9 times; sc in last 10 chs. Fasten off.

Row 2 (RS): Hold piece with RS facing you; sk first sc, with A make slip knot on hook and join with sc in next sc; sc in next 8 sc, in next ch-2 sp work (sc, ch 2, sc); *sc in next 8 sc, sk next sc, sc in next dc, sk next sc, sc in next 8 sc, in next ch-2 sp work (sc, ch 2, sc); rep from * 9 times; sc in next 9 sc. Fasten off, leaving last sc unworked.

Row 3: Hold piece with WS facing you; sk first sc, with B make slip knot on hook and join with sc in next sc; *sc in next 7 sc, ch 1, sk next sc, in next ch-2 sp work (sc, ch 2, sc); ch 1, sk next sc, sc in next 7 sc, sk next sc, sc in next sc, sk next sc; rep from * 9 times; sc in next 7 sc, ch 1, sk next sc, in next ch-2 sp work (sc, ch 2, sc); ch 1, sk next sc, sc in next 8 sc. Fasten off, leaving last sc unworked.

Row 4: Hold piece with RS facing you; sk first sc, with A make slip knot on hook and join with sc in next sc; *sc in next 6 sc, working in front of next ch-1 sp, dc in next sk st on 2nd row below, sc in next sc, in next ch-2 sp work (sc, ch 2, sc); sc in next sc, working in front of next ch-1 sp, dc in next sk st on 2nd row below, sc in next 6 sc, sk next sc, sc in next sc, sk next sc; rep from * 9 times; sc in next 6 sc, working in front of next ch-1 sp, dc in next sk st on 2nd row below, sc in next sc, in next ch-2 sp work (sc, ch 2, sc); sc in next sc, working in front of next ch-1 sp, dc in next sk st on 2nd row below, sc in next 7 sc. Fasten off, leaving last sc unworked.

Row 5: Hold piece with WS facing you; sk first sc, with B make slip knot on hook and join with sc in next sc; *sc in next 5 sc, ch 1, sk next dc, sc in next sc, ch 1, in next ch-2 sp work (sc, ch 2, sc); ch 1, sk next sc, sc in next sc, ch 1, sk next st, sc in next 5 sc, sk next sc, sc in next sc, sk next sc; rep from * 9 times; sc in next 5 sc, ch 1, sk next dc, sc in next sc, ch 1, in next ch-2 sp work (sc, ch 2, sc); ch 1, sk next sc, sc in next sc, ch 1, sk next dc, sc in next 6 sc. Fasten off, leaving last sc unworked.

Row 6: Hold piece with RS facing you; sk first sc, with A make slip knot on hook and join with sc in next sc; *sc in next 4 sc, [working in front of next ch-1 sp, dc in next sk dc on 2nd row below, sc in next sc] twice; in next ch-2 sp work (sc, ch 2, sc); [sc in next sc, working in front of next ch-1 sp, dc in next sk dc on 2nd row below] twice; sc in next 4 sc, sk next sc, sc in next sc, sk next sc; rep from * 9 times; sc in next 4 sc, [working in front of next ch-1 sp, dc in next sk dc on 2nd row below, sc in next sc] twice; in next ch-2 sp work (sc, ch 2, sc); [sc in next sc, working in front of next ch-1 sp, dc in next sk dc on 2nd row below] twice; sc in next 5 sc. Fasten off, leaving last sc unworked.

Row 7: Hold piece with WS facing you; sk first sc, with B make slip knot on hook and join with sc in next sc; *sc in next 3 sc, ch 1, sk next st, [sc in next sc, ch 1, sk next st] twice; in next ch-2 sp work (sc, ch 2, sc); ch 1, sk next sc, [sc in next sc, ch 1, sk next st] twice; sc in next 3 sc, sk next sc, sc in next sc, sk next sc; rep from * 9 times; sc in next 3 sc, ch 1, sk next st, [sc in next sc, ch 1, sk next st] twice; in next ch-2 sp work (sc, ch 2, sc); ch 1, sk next sc, [sc in next sc, ch 1, sk next st] twice; sc in next 4 sc. Fasten off, leaving last sc unworked.

Row 8: Hold piece with RS facing you; sk first sc, with A make slip knot on hook and join with sc in next sc; *sc in next 2 sc, [working in front of next ch-1 sp, dc in next sk st on 2nd row below, sc in next sc] 3 times; in next ch-2 sp work (sc, ch 2, sc); [sc in next sc, working in front of next ch-1 sp, dc in next sk st on 2nd row below] 3 times; sc in next 2 sc, sk next sc, sc in next sc, sk next sc; rep from * 9 times; sc in next 2 sc, [working in front of next ch-1 sp, dc in next sk st on 2nd row below, sc in next sc] 3 times; in next ch-2 sp work (sc, ch 2, sc); [sc in next sc, working in front of next ch-1 sp, dc in next sk st on 2nd row below] 3 times; sc in next 3 sc. Fasten off, leaving last sc unworked.

Row 9: Hold piece with WS facing you; sk first sc, with B make slip knot on hook and join with sc in next sc; *sc in next sc, ch 1, sk next st, [sc in next sc, ch 1, sk next st] 3 times; in next ch-2 sp work (sc, ch 2, sc); ch 1, sk next st, [sc in next sc, ch 1, sk next st] 3 times; [sc in next sc, sk next sc] twice; rep from * 9 times; sc in next sc, ch 1, sk next st, [sc in next sc, ch 1, sk next st] 3 times; in next ch-2 sp work (sc, ch 2, sc); ch 1, sk next st, [sc in next sc, ch 1, sk next st] 3 times; sc in next 2 sc. Fasten off, leaving last sc unworked.

Row 10: Hold piece with RS facing you; sk first sc, with A make slip knot on hook and join with sc in next sc; *[working in front of next ch-1 sp, dc in next sk st on 2nd row below, sc in next sc] 4 times; in next ch-2 sp work (sc, ch 2, sc); [sc in next sc, working in front of next ch-1 sp, dc in next sk st on 2nd row below] 4 times; sk next sc, sc in next sc, sk next sc; rep from * 9 times; [working in front of next ch-1 sp, dc in next sk st on 2nd row below, sc in next sc] 4 times; in next ch-2 sp work (sc, ch 2, sc); [sc in next sc, working in front of next ch-1 sp, dc in next sk st

on 2nd row below] 4 times; sc in next sc. Fasten off, leaving last sc unworked.

Row 11: Hold piece with WS facing you; sk first sc, with B make slip knot on hook and join with sc in next dc, sc in next 8 sts, in next ch-2 sp work (sc, ch 2, sc); *sc in next 8 sts, sk next st, sc in next

st, sk next st, sc in next 8 sts, in next ch-2 sp work (sc, ch 2, sc); rep from * 9 times; sc in next 9 sts. Fasten off, leaving last sc unworked.

Rep rows 2–11 until piece measures approximately 48 inches from beg. Then rep rows 2–10.

Weave in all ends.

Edging

Hold afghan with RS facing you and last row worked to left; with B make slip knot on hook and join with sc in unused sc at end of first row; 2 sc in same row; working across side in unused sc at end of rows, sc in each rem row; mark last sc made; ch 1; working across last row, sc in first sc, ch 1, sc in next 9 sc, in next ch-2 sp work (sc, ch 2, sc); [sc in next 8 sc, sk next sc, sc in next sc, sk next sc, sc in next 8 sc, in next ch-2 sp work (sc, ch 2, sc)] 11 times; sc in next 9 sc, ch 1, sc in last sc, ch 1; working across next side in unused sc at end of rows, sc in next row and in each rem row to last row; 3 sc in last row. Fasten off.

Border

Hold piece with RS facing you; with B make slip knot on hook and join with sc in marked st; sc in next ch-1 sp, in next sc, in next ch-1 sp and in next 10 sc; 4 sc in next ch-2 sp; [sc in next 8 sc, sk next sc, sc in next sc, sk next sc, sc in next 8 sc, 4 sc in next ch-2 sp] 10 times; sc in next 10 sc, sc in next ch-1 sp, in next sc, in next ch-1 sp and in each sc across next side to last sc of Edging; in last sc work (2 sc, ch 1, 2 sc); working across next side in unused lps of beg ch, sc in next 9 lps, sk next 2 lps, sc in next 9 lps, [3 sc in next lp, sc in next 9 lps, sk next 2 lps, sc in next 9 lps] 10 times; working across next side, in first sc of work (2 sc, ch 1, 2 sc); sc in each rem sc to first sc; join with sl st in first sc.
Fasten off and weave in all ends. ●

Smiling Scallops

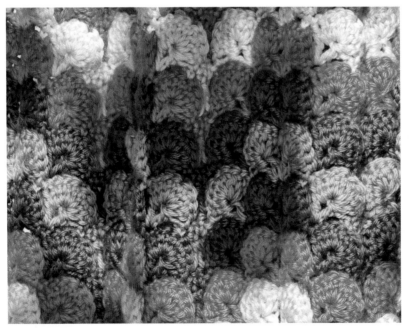

Skill Level
 EASY

Size
Approximately 44 x 54 inches

Materials
- Red Heart Soft Yarn medium (worsted) weight yarn (5 oz/256 yds/140g per skein):
    4 skeins #1882 toast (A)
    3 skeins #4422 tangerine (B)
    2 skeins each #4420 guacamole (C) and #4601 off-white (D)
- Size H/8/5mm crochet hook or size needed to obtain gauge
- Tapestry needle

Gauge

From point to point, 1 horizontal
pattern rep = 5¼ inches

Special Stitches

V-stitch (V-st): In st indicated work
(dc, ch 1, dc).

Cluster (cl): Keeping last lp of each
dc on hook, dc in st indicated, sk
next st, dc in next st, yo and draw
through all 3 lps on hook.

Shell: Dc in st indicated, 6 dc in
back lp (see Stitch Guide) of
same st.

Instructions

Center

Row 1 (RS): With A, ch 248 loosely;
dc in 5th ch from hook—beg cl
made; *[ch 1, sk next 2 chs, dc
in next ch, ch 1, sk next 2 chs, in
next ch work **V-st** (see Special
Stitches)] twice; ch 3, [in next ch
work V-st; ch 1, sk next 2 chs, dc
in next ch, ch 1, sk next 2 chs]
twice; **cl** (see Special Stitches) in
next 3 chs; rep from * across, turn.

Row 2: Ch 1, sc in first cl; *[sc in
next dc, sk next dc, **shell** (see
Special Stitches) in next ch, sk
next dc] twice; 2 sc in next ch-3
sp; [sk next dc, shell in next ch,
sk next dc, sc in next dc] twice;
sc in next cl; rep from * 7 times;
[sc in next dc, sk next dc, shell in
next ch, sk next dc] twice; 2 sc in
next ch-3 sp; [sk next dc, shell in
next ch, sk next dc, sc in next dc]
twice; sc in next dc. Fasten off,
leaving beg 4 sk chs unworked.

Row 3: Hold piece with RS facing
you; with C make slip knot on
hook; yo; holding yo with index
finger, insert hook in first sc, yo,
draw up lp, yo, draw through 2
lps on hook; yo, insert hook in
next sc, yo, draw up lp, yo, draw
through 2 lps on hook, yo and
draw through all 3 lps on hook—
beg dc dec made; *[ch 1, sk next 3
dc, sc in next dc, ch 1, sk next 3 dc,
V-st in next sc] twice; ch 3, [V-st
in next sc, ch 1, sk next 3 dc, sc in

next dc, ch 1, sk next 3 dc] twice;
cl in next 3 sc; rep from * 7 times;
[ch 1, sk next 3 dc, sc in next dc,
ch 1, sk next 3 dc, V-st in next sc]
twice; ch 3, [V-st in next dc, ch 1,
sk next 3 dc, sc in next dc, ch 1, sk
next 3 dc] twice; **dc dec** (see Stitch
Guide) in next 2 sts, turn.

Row 4: Ch 1, sc in first st; *[sc in
next sc, sk next dc, shell in next
ch, sk next dc] twice; 2 sc in
next ch-3 sp; [sk next dc, shell
in next ch, sk next dc, sc in next
sc] twice; sc in next st; rep from *
across. Fasten off.

Rows 5 & 6: With A, rep rows 3
and 4.

Rows 7 & 8: With B, rep rows 3
and 4.

Rows 9 & 10: With D, rep rows 3
and 4.

Rows 11 & 12: With B, rep rows 3
and 4.

Rows 13 & 14: With A, rep rows 3
and 4.

Rep rows 3–14 until piece measures
approximately 52 inches from
beg. Then rep rows 3–6.

Weave in all ends. ●

Seaside Waves

Skill Level

 EASY

Size

Approximately 30 x 49 inches

Materials

- Red Heart Classic medium (worsted) weight yarn (3½ oz/190yds/99g per skein):
    - 5 skeins #653 medium teal (A)
    - 2 skeins #622 pale sage (B)
- Red Heart Super Saver medium (worsted) weight yarn (7 oz/364 yds/198g per skein):
    - 2 skeins #657 dusty teal (C)
- Size H/8/5mm crochet hook or size needed to obtain gauge
- Tapestry needle
- Stitch marker

Gauge

From point to point, 1 horizontal pattern rep = 5 inches

Special Stitch

Cluster (cl): Ch 3, yo, insert hook in 3rd ch from hook, yo and draw lp through, yo, draw through 2 lps on hook, yo, insert hook in same ch, yo and draw lp through, yo, draw through 2 lps on hook, yo and draw through all 3 lps on hook.

Instructions

Center

Row 1 (RS): With A, ch 159 loosely; sc in 5th ch from hook *(beg 4 sk chs count as a dc and a ch-1 sp)*; *[ch 1, sk next ch, sc in next ch] 5 times; [ch 1, sc in next ch] twice; [ch 1, sk next ch, sc in next ch] 5 times; sk next ch, dc in next ch, sk next ch, sc in next ch; rep from * 4 times; [ch 1, sk next ch, sc in next ch] 5 times; [ch 1, sc in next ch] twice; [ch 1, sk next ch, sc in next ch] 5 times; sk next ch, dc in next ch. Fasten off.

Row 2: Hold piece with WS facing you; with C make slip knot on hook and join with sc in first dc; *ch 3, sk next 4 sts, sc in next sc, ch 3, sk next 3 sts, sc in next sc, ch 3, sk next 2 sts, sc in next ch, ch 3, sk next sc, sc in next ch, ch 3, sk next 2 sts, sc in next sc, ch 3, sk next 3 sts, sc in next sc, ch 3, sk next 4 sts, sc in next dc; rep from * 4 times; ch 3, sk next 4 sts, sc in next sc, ch 3, sk next 3 sts, sc in next sc, ch 3, sk next 2 sts, sc in next ch, ch 3, sk next sc, sc in next ch, ch 3, sk next 2 sts, sc in next sc, ch 3, sk next 3 sts, sc in next sc, ch 3, sk next 4 sts, sc in 3rd ch of beg 4 sk chs. Fasten off.

Row 3: Hold piece with RS facing you; with A make slip knot on hook and join with sc in first sc; *working behind next ch-3 sp, sk next 2 sk sts on 2nd row below, dc in next sk st, ch 1, sc in next sc, ch 1, [working behind next ch-3 sp, sk next sk st on 2nd row below, dc in next sk st, ch 1, sc in next sc, ch 1] twice; working behind next ch-3 sp, dc in next sk sc on 2nd row below, ch 1, sc in next sc, ch 1, working behind next ch-3 sp, dc in next sk st on 2nd row below, [ch 1, sc in next sc, ch 1, working behind next ch-3 sp, sk next st on 2nd row below, dc in next sk st] twice;

sc in next sc; rep from * across. Fasten off.

Row 4: Hold piece with WS facing you; with C make slip knot on hook and join with sc in first sc; *ch 3, sk next 4 sts, sc in next dc, ch 3, sk next 3 sts, sc in next dc, ch 3, sk next 2 sts, sc in next ch, ch 3, sk next dc, sc in next ch, ch 3, sk next 2 sts, sc in next dc, ch 3, sk next 3 sts, sc in next dc, ch 3, sk next 4 sts, sc in next sc; rep from * across. Fasten off.

Row 5: Hold piece with RS facing you; with A make slip knot on hook and join with sc in first sc; *[working behind next ch-3 sp, dc in next sk sc on 2nd row below, ch 1, sc in next sc, ch 1] 3 times; working behind next ch-3 sp, dc in next sk dc on 2nd row below, [ch 1, sc in next sc, ch 1, working behind next ch-3 sp, dc in next sk sc on 2nd row below] 3 times; sc in next sc; rep from * across. Fasten off.

Row 6: Hold piece with WS facing you; with B, make slip knot on hook and join with sc in first sc; ch 3, sk next 4 sts, sc in next dc; *ch 3, sk next 3 sts, sc in next dc, ch 3, sk next 2 sts, sc in next ch, ch 3, sk next dc, sc in next ch, ch 3, sk next 2 sts, sc in next dc, ch 3, sk next 3 sts, sc in next dc, cl *(see Special Stitch)*; ch 1, sk next 4 sts, sc in next sc, cl; ch 1, sk next 4 sts, sc in next dc; rep from * 8 times; ch 3, sk next 3 sts, sc in next dc, ch 3, sk next 2 sts, sc in next ch, ch 3, sk next dc, sc in next ch, ch 3, sk next 2 sts, sc in next dc, ch 3, sk next 3 sts, sc in next dc, ch 3, sk next 4 sts, sc in last sc. Fasten off.

   American School of Needlework • Berne, Indiana 46711 • DRGnetwork.com

Row 7: Hold piece with RS facing you; with A make slip knot on hook and join with sc in first sc; *[working behind next ch-3 sp or cl, dc in next sk sc on 2nd row below, ch 1, sc in next sc, ch 1] 3 times; working behind next ch-3 sp, dc in next sk dc on 2nd row below, [ch 1, sc in next sc, ch 1, working behind next ch-3 sp or cl, dc in next sk sc on 2nd row below] 3 times; sc in next sc; rep from * across. Fasten off.

Rows 8 & 9: Rep rows 6 and 7.

Rows 10 & 11: Rep rows 4 and 5.

Rep rows 4–11 until piece measures approximately 48 inches from beg.

Rep row 4.

Weave in all ends.

Edging

Hold afghan with RS facing you and last row worked to left; with A make slip knot on hook and join with sc in base of beg 4 sk chs of first row, sc in same sp; ch 1, sc in 3rd ch of same beg 4 sk chs; ch 1, working across side in ends of rows, *sk next row, sc in next row, ch 1; rep from * to last row; mark last ch-1 sp made; working across last row worked, sc in first sc, ch 1; **[working behind next ch-3 sp, dc in next sk sc on 2nd row below, ch 1, sc in next sc, ch 1] 3 times; working behind next ch-3 sp, dc in next sk dc on 2nd row below, [ch 1, sc in next sc, ch 1, working behind next ch-3 sp, dc in next sk sc on 2nd row below] 3 times; sc in next sc; rep from ** 7 times; [working behind next ch-3 sp, dc in next sk sc on 2nd row below, ch 1, sc in next sc, ch 1] 3 times; working behind next ch-3 sp, dc in next sk dc on 2nd row below, [ch 1, sc in next sc, ch 1, working behind next ch-3 sp, dc in next sk sc on 2nd row below] 3 times; ch 1, sc in last sc, ch 1, working across next side in end of rows, sk first row; ***sc in next row, ch 1, sk next row; rep from *** to last row; sc in top of dc at end of row, ch 1, 2 sc in unused lp of ch at base of same dc.

Fasten off and weave in ends.

Border

Hold piece with RS facing you; with A make slip knot on hook and join with sc in marked ch-1 sp; ch 2, sl st in next ch-1 sp, [ch 1, sl st in next ch-1 sp] 6 times; ch 2, sl st in next ch-1 sp, *[ch 1, sl st in next ch-1 sp] 5 times; sk next st, sl st in next sc, [ch 1, sl st in next ch-1 sp] 6 times; ch 2, sl st in next ch-1 sp; rep from * 8 times; [ch 1, sl st in next ch-1 sp] 6 times; ch 2, sl st in next ch-1 sp, [ch 1, sl st in next ch-1 sp] across to last 2 sc of rnd 1; ch 1, sk next sc, in last sc work (sl st, ch 2, sl st); working in unused lps and sps of beg ch, [ch 1, sl st in next lp] 6 times; sk next ch, sl st in next ch, [ch 1, sl st in next sp] 6 times; ch 2, sl st in next sp, [ch 1, sl st in next sp] 5 times; sk next ch, sl st in next ch, [ch 1, sl st in next sp] 6 times] 9 times; ch 1, in first sc of rnd 1 work (sl st, ch 2, sl st); ch 1, sk next sc, [sl st in next ch-1 sp, ch 1] across to first sl st; join with sl st in first sl st.

Fasten off and weave in ends. ●

Rain or Shine

Skill Level

 EASY

Size

Approximately 32 x 54 inches
Note: This afghan is sized to cover both legs when seated.

Materials

- Red Heart Super Saver medium (worsted) weight yarn (7 oz/364 yds/196g per skein):
    - 3 skeins #365 coffee *(A)*
    - 1 skein each #358 lavender *(B)*, #530 orchid *(C)*, #778 lt. fuchsia *(D)* and #347 lt. periwinkle *(E)*
- Red Heart Classic medium (worsted) weight yarn (3½ oz/190 yds/99g per skein):
    - 2 skeins each #730 grenadine *(F)* and #822 true blue *(G)*
- Size H/8/5mm crochet hook or size needed to obtain gauge
- Tapestry needle

Gauge

From point to point, 3 horizontal pattern rep = 11½ inches

Special Stitch

Cluster (cl): Keeping last lp of each dc on hook, dc in 2 sts indicated on 1 row below, yo and draw through all 3 lps on hook.

Instructions

Center

Row 1 (RS): With A, ch 162 loosely; sc in 2nd ch from hook and in next 9 chs, ch 3, sk next ch; *sc in next 8 chs, draw up lp in next ch, sk next ch, draw up lp in next ch, yo and draw through all 3 lps on hook; sc in next 8 chs, ch 3, sk next ch; rep from * 6 times; sc in next 10 chs. Fasten off.

Row 2: Hold piece with WS facing you; sk first sc, with B make slip knot on hook and join with sc in next sc; [sc in next sc, ch 1, sk next st] 4 times; in next ch-3 sp work (sc, ch 3, sc); *ch 1, [sk next st, sc in next sc, ch 1] 3 times; sk next 2 sts, sc in next st, ch 1, sk next 2 sts, [sc in next sc, ch 1, sk next sc] 3 times; in next ch-3 sp work (sc, ch 3, sc); rep from * 6 times; ch 1, sk next st, [sc in next sc, ch 1, sk next st] 3 times; sc in next 2 sts. Fasten off, leaving rem sc unworked.

Row 3: Hold piece with RS facing you; sk first sc, with A make slip knot on hook and join with sc in next sc; [working behind next ch-1 sp, dc in sk st 1 row below, sc in next sc] 4 times; working behind next ch-3 sp, in next ch-3 sp 1 row below work (dc, ch 3, dc); on working row, sc in next sc; *[working behind next st, dc in next sk st 1 row below, on working row, sc in next sc] 3 times; working behind next 2 ch-1 sps, **cl** *(see Special Stitches)* in first sk st 1 row below and in 4th sk st 1 row below; sc in next sc, [working behind next ch-1 sp, dc in sk st 1 row below, sc in next sc]

3 times; working behind next ch-3 sp, in next ch-3 sp 1 row below work (dc, ch 3, dc); sc in next sc; rep from * 6 times; [working behind next ch-1 sp, dc in sk st 1 row below, sc in next sc] 4 times. Fasten off, leaving last sc unworked.

Row 4: With C, rep row 2.
Row 5: Rep row 3.
Rows 6 & 7: Rep rows 2 and 3.
Row 8: With D, rep row 2.
Row 9: Rep row 3.
Row 10: With F, rep row 2.
Row 11: Rep row 3.
Row 12: With D, rep row 2.
Row 13: Rep row 3.
Row 14: With G, rep row 2.
Row 15: Rep row 3.
Row 16: With E, rep row 2.
Row 17: Rep row 3.
Row 18: With G, rep row 2.
Row 19: Rep row 3.
Rows 20–127: [Work rows 2–19] 6 times.
Rows 128–144: Rep rows 2–6. Weave in all ends.

Edging

Hold afghan with RS facing you and last row worked at top; beg at lower right corner; working across side in top 2 lps of unworked sc at end of rows, with A make slip knot on hook and join with sc in first row; 2 sc in same row; sc in next row and in each row across to last row; mark last sc made; ch 1; working across top row, sc in first sc, ch 1, sc in next sc, [working behind next ch, dc in sk st 1 row below, sc in next sc] 4 times; working behind next ch-3 sp, in ch-3 sp 1 row below work (dc, ch 1, dc, ch 1, dc); sc in next

American School of Needlework • Berne, Indiana 46711 • DRGnetwork.com

sc; *[working behind next ch, dc in sk st 1 row below, sc in next sc] 3 times; yo, working behind next ch, insert hook in first sk st 1 row below, draw up lp, yo, draw through 2 lps on hook; yo, working behind next ch, insert hook in 2nd sk st 1 row below, draw up lp, yo, draw through 2 lps on hook, yo and draw through all 3 lps on hook (counts as 1 st); sc in next sc, [working behind next ch, dc in sk st 1 row below, sc in next sc] 3 times; working behind next ch-3 sp in ch-3 sp 1 row below work (dc, ch 1, dc, ch 1, dc); sc in next sc; rep from * 6 times; [working behind next ch, dc in sk st 1 row below, sc in next sc] 4 times; ch 1, sc in next sc, ch 1, working across next side in top 2 lps of unworked sc at end of rows, sc in next row and in each row across to last row; 3 sc in last row. Fasten off and weave in ends.

Border

Hold piece with RS facing you; with A make slip knot on hook and join with sc in marked st; sc in next ch-1 sp, in next sc, in next ch-1 sp, in next 10 sts and in next ch-1 sp, 3 sc in next dc; sc in next ch-1 sp, *sc in next 7 sts, sk next sc, sc in next sc, sk next sc, sc in next 7 sts and in next ch-1 sp, 3 sc in next dc, sc in next ch-1 sp; rep from * 6 times; sc in next 10 sts, sc in next ch-1 sp, in next sc, in next ch-1 sp, in next sc and in each sc across next side to last sc of Edging; in last sc work (sc, ch 1, 2 sc); working across next side in unused lps of beg ch, sc in next 9 lps, sk next lp, sc in next ch-1 sp, sk next lp, sc in next 8 lps; **3 sc in next lp, sc in next 8 lps, sk next lp, sc in next ch-1 sp, sk next lp, sc in next 8 lps; rep from ** 6 times; sc in last lp, in first sc of rnd 1 work (2 sc, ch 1, sc); sc in next sc and in each rem sc to first sc; join with sl st in first sc. Fasten off and weave in ends. ●

General Information

Standard Yarn Weight System
Categories of yarn, gauge ranges, and recommended hook sizes

Yarn Weight Symbol & Category Names	1 SUPER FINE	2 FINE	3 LIGHT	4 MEDIUM	5 BULKY	6 SUPER BULKY
Type of Yarns in Category	Sock, Fingering, Baby	Sport, Baby	DK, Light Worsted	Worsted, Afghan, Aran	Chunky, Craft, Rug	Bulky, Roving
Crochet Gauge* Ranges in Single Crochet to 4 inch	21–32 sts	16–20 sts	12–17 sts	11–14 sts	8–11 sts	5–9 sts
Recommended Hook in Metric Size Range	2.25–3.25mm	3.5–4.5mm	4.5–5.5mm	5.5–6.5mm	6.5–9mm	9mm and larger
Recommended Hook U.S. Size Range	B/1–E/4	E/4–7	7–I/9	I/9–K/10½	K/10½–M/13	M/13 and larger

* **GUIDELINES ONLY:** The above reflect the most commonly used gauges and hook sizes for specific yarn categories.

Skill Levels

BEGINNER
Beginner projects for first-time crocheters using basic stitches. Minimal shaping.

EASY
Easy projects using basic stitches, repetitive stitch patterns, simple color changes and simple shaping and finishing.

INTERMEDIATE
Intermediate projects with a variety of stitches, mid-level shaping and finishing.

EXPERIENCED
Experienced projects using advanced techniques and stitches, detailed shaping and refined finishing.

How to Check Gauge

A correct stitch-gauge is very important. Please take the time to work a stitch-gauge swatch about 4 x 4 inches. Measure the swatch. If the number of stitches and rows is fewer than indicated under "Gauge" in the pattern, your hook is too large. Try another swatch with a smaller size hook. If the number of stitches and rows is more than indicated under "Gauge" in the pattern, your hook is too small. Try another swatch with a larger size hook.

Symbols

* An asterisk (or double asterisk **) is used to mark the beginning of a portion of instructions to be worked more than once; thus, "rep from * twice more" means after working the instructions once, repeat the instructions following the asterisk twice more (3 times in all).

[] Brackets are used to enclose instructions that should be worked the exact number of times specified immediately following the brackets, such as "[2 sc in next dc, sc in next dc] twice."

[] Brackets and () parentheses are used to provide additional information to clarify instructions.

Stitch Guide

For more complete information, visit **AnniesAttic.com**

Abbreviations

beg	begin/beginning
bpdc	back post double crochet
bpsc	back post single crochet
bptr	back post treble crochet
CC	contrasting color
ch	chain stitch
ch-	refers to chain or space previously made (i.e., ch-1 space)
ch sp	chain space
cl	cluster
cm	centimeter(s)
dc	double crochet
dec	decrease/decreases/decreasing
dtr	double treble crochet
fpdc	front post double crochet
fpsc	front post single crochet
fptr	front post treble crochet
g	gram(s)
hdc	half double crochet
inc	increase/increases/increasing
lp(s)	loop(s)
MC	main color
mm	millimeter(s)
oz	ounce(s)
pc	popcorn
rem	remain/remaining
rep	repeat(s)
rnd(s)	round(s)
RS	right side
sc	single crochet
sk	skip(ped)
sl st	slip stitch
sp(s)	space(s)
st(s)	stitch(es)
tog	together
tr	treble crochet
trtr	triple treble crochet
WS	wrong side
yd(s)	yard(s)
yo	yarn over

Chain—ch: Yo, pull through lp on hook.

Slip stitch—sl st: Insert hook in st, pull through both lps on hook.

Single crochet—sc: Insert hook in st, yo, pull through st, yo, pull through both lps on hook.

Front post stitch—fp: Back post stitch—bp: When working post st, insert hook from right to left around post st on previous row.

Single crochet decrease (sc dec): (Insert hook, yo, draw lp through) in each of the sts indicated, yo, draw through all lps on hook.

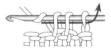

Example of 2-sc dec

Half double crochet decrease (hdc dec): (Yo, insert hook, yo, draw lp through) in each of the sts indicated, yo, draw through all lps on hook.

Example of 2-hdc dec

Double crochet decrease (dc dec): (Yo, insert hook, yo, draw loop through, draw through 2 lps on hook) in each of the sts indicated, yo, draw through all lps on hook.

Example of 2-dc dec

Front loop—front lp Back loop— back lp

Front Loop   Back Loop

Half double crochet— hdc: Yo, insert hook in st, yo, pull through st, yo, pull through all 3 lps on hook.

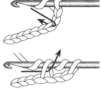

Double crochet—dc: Yo, insert hook in st, yo, pull through st, [yo, pull through 2 lps] twice.

Change colors: Drop first color; with 2nd color, pull through last 2 lps of st.

Treble crochet—tr: Yo twice, insert hook in st, yo, pull through st, [yo, pull through 2 lps] 3 times.

Double treble crochet—dtr: Yo 3 times, insert hook in st, yo, pull through st, [yo, pull through 2 lps], 4 times.

Treble crochet decrease (tr dec): Holding back last lp of each st, tr in each of the sts indicated, yo, pull through all lps on hook.

US		UK
sl st (slip stitch)	=	sc (single crochet)
sc (single crochet)	=	dc (double crochet)
hdc (half double crochet)	=	htr (half treble crochet)
dc (double crochet)	=	tr (treble crochet)
tr (treble crochet)	=	dtr (double treble crochet)
dtr (double treble crochet)	=	ttr (triple treble crochet)
skip	=	miss

Inches Into Millimeters & Centimeters

All measurements are rounded off slightly.

inches	mm	cm	inches	cm	inches	cm	inches	cm
⅛	3	0.3	5	12.5	21	53.5	38	96.5
¼	6	0.6	5½	14	22	56.0	39	99.0
⅜	10	1.0	6	15.0	23	58.5	40	101.5
½	13	1.3	7	18.0	24	61.0	41	104.0
⅝	15	1.5	8	20.5	25	63.5	42	106.5
¾	20	2.0	9	23.0	26	66.0	43	109.0
⅞	22	2.2	10	25.5	27	68.5	44	112.0
1	25	2.5	11	28.0	28	71.0	45	114.5
1¼	32	3.8	12	30.5	29	73.5	46	117.0
1½	38	3.8	13	33.0	30	76.0	47	119.5
1¾	45	4.5	14	35.5	31	79.0	48	122.0
2	50	5.0	15	38.0	32	81.5	49	124.5
2½	65	6.5	16	40.5	33	84.0	50	127.0
3	75	7.5	17	43.0	34	86.5		
3½	90	9.0	18	46.0	35	89.0		
4	100	10.0	19	48.5	36	91.5		
4½	115	11.5	20	51.0	37	94.0		

Crochet Hooks Conversion Chart

U.S.	1/B	2/C	3/D	4/E	5/F	6/G	8/H	9/I	10/J	10½/K	N
Continental-mm	2.25	2.75	3.25	3.5	3.75	4.25	5	5.5	6	6.5	9.0

American School of Needlework ®
excellence in instruction

TOLL-FREE ORDER LINE or to request a free catalog (800) 582-6643
Customer Service (800) 282-6643, **Fax** (800) 882-6643
Visit DRGnetwork.com.

We have made every effort to ensure the accuracy and completeness of these instructions.
We cannot, however, be responsible for human error, typographical mistakes or variations in individual work.

ISBN: 978-1-59012-212-9   All rights reserved.   Printed in USA   1 2 3 4 5 6 7 8 9